Great Minds of Science

Isaac Newton

The Greatest Scientist of All Time

Revised Edition

Margaret J. Anderson

Enslow Publishers, Inc.
40 Industrial Road
Box 398
Berkeley Heights, NJ 07922
USA

http://www.enslow.com

Library of Congress Cataloging-in-Publication Data

Anderson, Margaret Jean, 1931-
  Isaac Newton: the greatest scientist of all time / Margaret J. Anderson.—
Rev. ed.
     p. cm.—(Great minds of science)
  Summary: "A biography of English scientist and mathematician Isaac
Newton"—Provided by publisher.
  Includes bibliographical references and index.
  ISBN-13: 978-0-7660-2793-0
  ISBN-10: 0-7660-2793-7
  1. Newton, Isaac, Sir, 1642-1727—Juvenile literature. 2. Physicists—Great
Britain—Biography—Juvenile literature. I. Title.
  QC16.N7A53 2008
  530.092—dc22
  [B]

                              2007029382

Printed in the United States of America

10 9 8 7 6 5 4 3 2 1

To Our Readers: We have done our best to make sure all Internet addresses in
this book were active and appropriate when we went to press. However, the
author and the publisher have no control over and assume no liability for
the material available on those Internet sites or on other Web sites they may
link to. Any comments or suggestions can be sent by e-mail to
comments@enslow.com or to the address on the back cover.

Illustration Credits: Margaret J. Anderson, pp. 6, 9, 12, 14, 18, 20, 30, 33, 42,
56, 63, 70, 81, 87, 96; National Photographic Library/Derick E. Witty/The
Image Works, p. 7; Stephen Delisle, pp. 25, 36, 39, 45, 48, 76, 116, 117; The
Granger Collection, New York, pp. 29, 38, 65, 66, 92, 106; Jupiterimages
Corporation/Photos.com, pp. 51, 80, 99, 101.

Cover Illustration: Lexy Sinnott/Shutterstock, Inc. (Background); National
Photographic Library/Derick E. Witty/The Image Works (Inset).

Contents

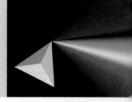

"A Sober, Silent, Thinking Lad"

ON CHRISTMAS DAY 1642, HANNAH Newton gave birth to a baby boy. She named him Isaac after his father, but there was no father on hand to welcome the new baby. Hannah's husband had died in October.

Little Isaac was born early. He was so small that his mother later said she could have fit him inside a quart jug. He was so weak that she had to fix a little pillow around his neck to hold up his head. Two women, who were helping Hannah on the day her son was born, were sent to a neighbor's house to fetch some medicine. They saw no need to hurry. They were so sure that Isaac would not live until they got back that they rested on a wall.[1]

This baby, who got off to such a shaky start,

Isaac Newton was born on Christmas Day 1642, in Woolsthorpe Manor.

grew up to have one of the best minds of all time. Isaac Newton was a genius. Before he was out of college, he had invented a branch of mathematics called calculus. He had designed the reflecting telescope. He had figured out the principle of gravity. And he had proved that white light contains all the colors of the rainbow.

Isaac Newton's genius cannot be explained

Isaac Newton had one of the greatest
scientific minds of all time.

by his family background. His father, like his father before him, was a simple farmer. In his will, he left Woolsthorpe Manor in Lincolnshire to his wife. The will was signed with an X. He did not know how to write his own name. Hannah's side of the family had more education. Hannah knew how to write. Her two brothers were clergymen and had been to college.

Nor can Isaac's genius be explained by his upbringing. He seems to have been a lonely child. Woolsthorpe Manor was a modest farmhouse in the country. A number of relatives lived in the area, but we do not know whether or not they came to visit.

Childhood Years

When Isaac was three years old, Hannah married again. Her new husband was a clergyman named Barnabas Smith. He lived in a village about a mile and a half from Woolsthorpe Manor. Smith was much older than Hannah, but he was wealthy and well educated.

This is a replica of the sundial that Isaac Newton carved on a wall when he was nine years old.

It was a good match for the young widow, but things did not go well for Isaac. The little boy was left behind at Woolsthorpe Manor. His grandmother moved in to take care of him. When he was around five, he went to the village school, where he learned to read and write.

Isaac had his own bedroom in the attic. He carved figures on the wooden windowsill.

Sometimes he amused himself by drawing on the walls. One sketch, done when he was nine, shows the beginning of his genius. He marked out a sundial on a wall.

The following year, Isaac's stepfather died and his mother returned to Woolsthorpe. She did not come alone; she now had three more children. Mary was four and a half, Benjamin was two, and little Hannah was one.

Two years later, Isaac was sent off to grammar school in Grantham. Grantham was a market town, seven miles from Woolsthorpe. Seven miles was too far for Isaac to travel each day, so he boarded with the Clark family. They lived on High Street next to the George Inn. Mr. Clark ran an apothecary shop (drugstore). By watching Mr. Clark prepare medicines, Isaac learned some chemistry. This was helpful to him later on. He also gathered herbs and learned their uses.

Mrs. Clark had two sons and a daughter from an earlier marriage. Isaac did not get along with the boys, Edward and Arthur Storer. He preferred the daughter's company. Some of what we know about Newton's boyhood is from her memories. When she was eighty-two, she was interviewed by William Stukeley, who was writing Isaac Newton's biography. She said that Isaac was always a "sober, silent, thinking lad." She remembered him making "little tables . . . and other utensils, for her, and her play fellows, to set their babys and trinkets on."[2]

Isaac is said to have "entertain'd a passion for her when they grew up."[3] Miss Storer is the only hint of a romance in Isaac's long life, and we do not even know her first name. He remained friendly with her over the years. After she married, whenever Isaac was in Grantham, he visited her and her husband.

Grammar School

Isaac did not get along any better with the boys at school than he did with the Storer brothers at home. He was still small for his age, and he was used to being alone. His schoolmates found him "too cunning."[4] He seldom joined them in their

Newton attended the Grantham Grammar School.

games. When he did, he tried to make sure he won. One windy day, the boys held a jumping contest. Isaac timed his jump to match an extra-strong gust of wind and set a record. He was already putting physics to work!

Isaac also used his cunning in making kites. He figured out the best place to fasten the string and how long the tail should be. One time he tied a paper lantern with a candle in it to the tail of a kite. He flew it in the dark and "wonderfully affrighted" the neighbors.[5] They talked about the strange light over their mugs of ale.

Mr. Stokes, the schoolmaster, was a good teacher. But Isaac did not do well in his new school. He sat at the bottom of the lowest class. Perhaps the village school had not prepared him for grammar school. More likely, he did not find the lessons interesting. In mathematics, students learned only basic arithmetic. Latin was a more important subject. Textbooks and scientific papers were all written in Latin. The Bible and Bible history were other important subjects.

Isaac did not study current affairs at school, although those were restless times. In 1642, a few months before Isaac's birth, King Charles I quarreled with Parliament. Oliver Cromwell, who was a Puritan, led a rebellion against the king. This led to a civil war that lasted six and a half years. King Charles was tried for treason and beheaded. Cromwell then became Lord

Charles I was executed in 1649 at the end of the English Civil War. Oliver Cromwell became the Lord Protector and ruled Britain for the next nine years.

Protector. He did not get along with Parliament any better than Charles had.

Isaac's attitude toward school suddenly changed after a fight with Arthur Storer. One morning, Arthur kicked him in the stomach. This led to a scuffle in the churchyard after school. Isaac was smaller than Arthur, but he had more spirit. He came out the clear winner. But that was not enough for Isaac. He decided to beat his rival in schoolwork as well. He began to study hard and soon rose to the top of the class.

Isaac still liked to draw. His attic room was decorated with sketches of birds, beasts, men, ships, and plants. He drew shapes, such as circles and triangles. No one seems to have minded. The drawings were not scrubbed off. He also made sundials all over the Clarks' house. He marked the hours, the half hours, and the quarter hours with pegs. He tied strings between the pegs to measure the shadows on different days. He could tell the shortest and longest days and the time of the equinoxes.

Isaac was aware of the movement of shadows all his life. When he walked into a sunny room, he could tell the time from the position of shadows without looking at a clock. But this did not keep him from being interested in clocks. While he lived with the Clarks, he made a water clock. It worked by dripping water through a small hole. It kept good time unless the hole was "furr'd up [blocked] by impuritys in the water."[6]

One day, after watching the construction of a wind-powered mill on the edge of town, Isaac went home and built a scale model. He used cloth for sails. Instead of wind power, he used a treadmill run by a mouse to turn the sails. People dropped in to see Isaac's "mouse miller."[7] A neighboring farmer provided Isaac with corn to feed his mouse.

Although Isaac was now doing well at school, his mother decided she needed him on the farm. It was time for her sixteen-year-old son to help with the work. So Isaac went home to Woolsthorpe Manor.

New Horizons

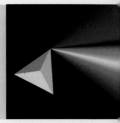

WHEN ISAAC RETURNED TO WOOLSTHORPE Manor, his mind was still on models and inventions. He had no interest in farming. Instead of watching the sheep, he built waterwheels in the brook. Meantime, the sheep caused trouble by eating the neighbor's grain.

On market days, Isaac often bribed his mother's servant to drop him off at the first corner past the manor. While the servant sold the produce and bought supplies, Isaac made models or read a book. When he did go into town, instead of keeping his mind on what he was supposed to be doing, he went over to the Clarks' house, where he spent the day reading in his old room.

The road outside Grantham was very steep.

Although Isaac Newton preferred reading to going to the market, a shopping center in Grantham bears his name.

Isaac usually led his horse up the hill. One day, when he reached the top, he forgot to mount again. He was so lost in thought that he walked on for the next five miles, leading the horse. Another time, when the horse slipped out of the bridle and went home by itself, Isaac did not even notice. He continued to trudge along with the empty bridle in his hand.

The servants thought that young Isaac was foolish, and his mother did not know what to do with him. Luckily, his old schoolmaster, Mr. Stokes, was now living in a nearby village. He told Hannah that her son's brain was wasted on a farm. He said that Isaac should go back to grammar school to fit himself for Cambridge University. He even offered to pay Isaac's fees and to give him a place to stay.

It was a good solution all around. Isaac was back among his beloved books. His mother could relax, and the servants "rejoic'd at parting with him, declaring, he was fit for nothing but the 'Versity."[1]

Cambridge University

Isaac Newton set off for Cambridge University in June 1661. The young man must have been both excited and nervous when he first saw the spires on the skyline. The buildings were impressive. They were old even then. There is no record of what Isaac thought, but we do know from his account book that it took him three

Trinity College of Cambridge University was founded in 1546 by Henry VIII.

days to get there. We also know that when he arrived, he spent money on supplies. He bought a lock for his desk, a notebook, ink, a pound of candles, and a chamber pot. Ink and candles often appear in Isaac's account book. He had a habit of staying up all night reading, studying, and taking notes.

Cambridge University is divided into

colleges. Isaac enrolled in Trinity College. He
started out as a sizar. Sizars paid lower fees and
acted as servants to the wealthier students
and teachers. It is rather surprising that Isaac
chose to be a sizar. His mother had a good
income. She owned Woolsthorpe Manor and
had inherited money and land from her second
husband, Barnabas Smith. She could have
afforded to pay her son's fees. Maybe she
thought Isaac would get more out of his
education if he worked for it. Maybe she was
annoyed that he had not chosen to be a farmer.

Being a sizar set Isaac apart from the other
students. He made no close friends, but then he
had made no close friends at grammar school,
either. Back in the seventeenth century, students
faced some of the same problems they do today.
Isaac had roommate troubles. He was studious,
but his roommate liked to have parties. One
evening, to get away from the noise, Isaac went
for a walk. While he was out, he met John
Wickins, and they began talking. They found
that both were wandering around in the dark for

the same reason. They were trying to get away from noisy roommates. The answer to their problem was plain: they agreed to "shake off their present disorderly Companions and Chum together."[2] Isaac Newton and John Wickins shared rooms for many years at Cambridge. They suited one another, yet they never became close friends.

Every student had a tutor who directed his studies. Isaac's tutor was Benjamin Pulleyn. In those days, universities did not offer a wide range of subjects. College prepared young men for a career in the church or in medicine. A third choice was to become a scholar and stay on at Cambridge as a fellow, or teacher.

Discovering Mathematics

Isaac's interest in mathematics was kindled by a visit to Sturbridge Fair. The fair—the biggest in England—came to Cambridge each August. Isaac purchased a book on astrology at one of the stalls. To help him understand the mathematics in his new book, he then bought a geometry text by Euclid, a Greek mathematician who had lived around 300 B.C. When Isaac first read Euclid, he did not think much of it. So he turned to a book by René Descartes. Descartes was a brilliant French mathematician, who had moved to the Netherlands where people were more open to new ideas. Isaac got bogged down in the math after a few pages. He went back to the beginning. This time he got three or four pages farther before he was stuck. Back he went to the beginning. He continued in this way until he had mastered the whole book.

The mathematics professor at Cambridge was a young man in his early thirties named Isaac Barrow. It was some time before he realized that Isaac Newton was a remarkable student. During an exam, Professor Barrow tested Isaac on what he knew about Euclid's geometry. Isaac could not answer his questions. He was too shy to say he had been busy reading Descartes's book on the new geometry. Even if Isaac had told Barrow this, the professor might not have believed him. Understanding Descartes without first reading Euclid would seem to be impossible. But Isaac Newton was remarkable at mathematics. While he was still a student, he developed the binomial theorem (rule). A binomial is two numbers connected by a plus or minus sign. Newton's rule provided a shortcut for multiplying a binomial by itself many times over. By the time he was twenty-two years old, Isaac was already going beyond other people's thinking.

The Note Taker

Isaac took notes on everything he read. These notes form part of a collection of Newton's papers, now at Cambridge University. From these papers we know what interested him during his student days. At one point, he changed his style of handwriting so that he could take notes faster. He wrote with a feather pen and figured out new ways of making ink. Soon after going to Cambridge, Isaac made a list of his sins. One of them was making a new pen on a Sunday.

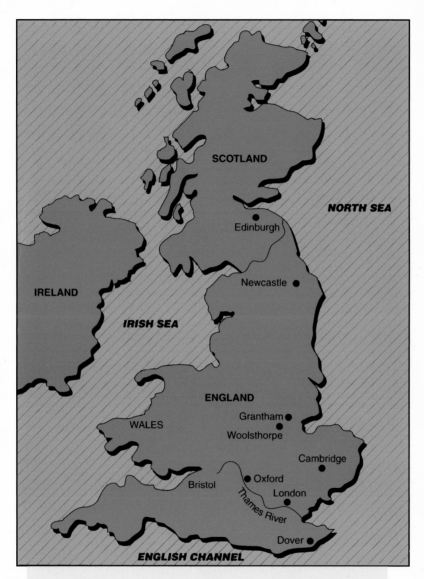

Isaac Newton spent his whole life in England. By the time of his death, he was known throughout Europe as a great scientist.

Isaac had a book where he wrote down things that he wanted to know more about. He listed forty-five headings. Some were about general subjects, such as matter, time, and motion. Headings like "Soul" and "Sleep" show how wide his interests were. Under "Of Water and Salt" he wrote about the tides. He came up with the theory that tides were connected with the phases of the moon. He explained their movement without ever having seen the ocean.

Isaac was fascinated by the night sky. One of the headings in his notebook was "Of the Sunn, Starrs & Planetts & Comets." He stayed up so many nights in 1664 watching a comet that he became "disordered."[3] He often forgot to eat. His cat was well fed on the food he left untouched on his plate. All his life, Isaac had the habit of thinking about something so deeply that he forgot to eat or sleep.

Some of his experiments put him in danger. Once, he stared with his right eye at the image of the sun in a mirror. When he closed his eye, he saw colored circles. He was interested in how the circles changed color as they faded, so he tried the experiment again, nearly ruining his eyesight. He began to see spots of color everywhere. He had to stay in a dark room for several days to recover his sight. This cured him of looking at the sun, but it did not cure him of experimenting with his own eyes. He did so again while trying to understand the nature of light.

In the spring of 1665, Isaac earned his bachelor of arts degree. He was one of twenty-six men earning degrees. We do not know how Isaac compared with these other students because the page in the book that shows the rankings of the students is missing. In his biography of Newton, William Stukeley claims that Isaac did not pass the first time. He had been too busy "in the solid track of learning" to study for the test.[4]

Isaac's next goal was his master of arts degree. However, in the summer of 1665, plague hit Cambridge and sent Isaac back home to Woolsthorpe. But the plague did not keep him from being a scholar. Isaac Newton's genius was about to burst into full bloom.

3

A Fruitful Vacation

TWO NATIONAL EVENTS TOOK PLACE IN the early 1660s that helped shape Isaac Newton's career. When Oliver Cromwell, the Lord Protector, died in 1658, his son Richard took over. Richard did not possess his father's strong character. He resigned after one year. England was ready to have a king again. Charles II was crowned in 1660.

Charles II took an active interest in advances in science. In 1662, he gave his backing to the founding of the Royal Society. Society meetings provided a setting where scientists could share their discoveries. In this way, they could keep up with new ideas. The first members of the Royal Society included the architect Christopher Wren and the writer Samuel Pepys. Robert Hooke, a

Charles II (1630–1685) was a strong supporter of science and the Royal Society.

The great plague caused many people to flee from London. The dead were laid out on the street. Wagons travelled the city picking up the victims. They were buried in mass graves.

brilliant physicist, was put in charge of doing experiments.

Toward the end of 1664, a serious illness broke out in London. It started out like the flu with a headache, high fever, and dizziness. This was followed by swellings in the armpits and on the neck. Within a few days, patients either died or recovered. Most died. The dreaded plague had surfaced again. There was good reason for fear. In the fourteenth century, an outbreak called the Black Death killed one in four people in Europe.

Plague is a disease of rats that is passed to people by fleas. Both rats and fleas thrived in the dirty, crowded conditions found in seventeenth-century London. The disease spread quickly. By the summer of 1665, it had claimed thirty-one thousand lives.

Samuel Pepys described the scenes of horror in his diary. Red crosses were painted on the doors of the houses of the sick. Carts were pushed through the street to the mournful cry of "Bring out your dead!" Charles II and his court left for the country. So did everyone else with somewhere to go. People fleeing London carried the sickness to other cities.

Gravity

By August 1665, the plague had reached Cambridge. The university closed its doors.

Many of the teachers and students had already left. Isaac Newton, who was now twenty-two years old, was at Woolsthorpe Manor. Back home, he studied harder than ever. His next eighteen months were later called "the miracle years." Newton did his greatest thinking during this time. Fifty years later, he said, "In those days I was in the prime of my age for invention and minded mathematics and philosophy more than any time since."[1]

The servants did not realize that Newton was "minding mathematics" while he sat in the garden under the apple tree. They probably thought he was as idle as ever. But his mind was busy. He was thinking about gravity. The story goes that while he was sitting in the garden, an apple fell from the tree. Why did the apple fall *down*, he wondered. Why not *up*, or *sideways*? He figured that some force must be pulling the apple toward the earth. Isaac Newton had discovered the principle of gravity.

Newton did not really figure out gravity in the time it takes an apple to fall from a tree,

This apple tree on the grounds of Woolsthorpe Manor is a direct descendant of Newton's famous tree.

though he himself gave us the apple legend. When he was an old man, he told the story to William Stukeley. They were drinking tea together under an apple tree in his garden. He said that he was sitting under a similar tree when the theory of gravity came to his mind. "It was occasion'd by the fall of an apple . . . "[2]

Calculus

For some time before the apple fell, Newton's thinking had been preparing him for the question of gravity. He was interested in the mathematics of motion. If something moves in a straight line at a constant speed, it is easy to figure out where it will be at any given time. For example, a car traveling along a straight road at fifty miles per hour will be fifty miles away at the end of an hour. But how do you figure out where the car will be if it speeds up or slows down? Where will it be if it is traveling around curves?

By using algebra, Newton could solve an equation to find the value of an unknown number, x. Finding the value of an unknown number that kept changing was a tougher problem. Newton set about looking for an answer. In doing so, he came up with a new branch of mathematics. He called it fluxions, from the word *flux*, which means "constant changing or flowing." We now call it calculus.

Late in the fall of 1665, Newton used fluxions to find the area under an open curve known as a hyperbola. The answer thrilled him so much that he took it to fifty-two places beyond the decimal. However, he did not rush out and tell everyone about this useful new branch of mathematics. Isaac Newton was always slow to share his discoveries with the world. He had to be sure he had everything right. Besides, he was impatient to explore the other new ideas that were crowding into his mind.

If Newton had told people about fluxions right away, he could have avoided a long quarrel. Ten years later, Wilhelm Leibniz came up with more or less the same method in Germany. A great many people were drawn into the argument about who should get the credit

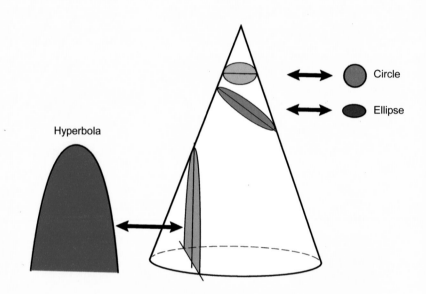

Circle

Ellipse

Hyperbola

Different shapes result from cutting a cone at different angles.

for inventing calculus. Newton can claim to be the first person to use calculus to solve problems in physics, but it is the symbols that Leibniz thought up that are in use today. As well as being used in every branch of physics, calculus is needed to solve problems in other fields, such as computer science, statistics, engineering, economics, and business. Without calculus, Albert Einstein could not have explained his theory of relativity.

Laws of Motion

Like many scientists before him, Isaac Newton was interested in the movement of the planets. The work of a German astronomer, Johannes Kepler, provided a starting point for his studies.

Kepler's three laws of motion state that:

1. Each planet travels in an ellipse around the sun. The sun is at one of the two focal points of the ellipse.

2. The speed of a planet traveling around the sun changes all the time. It changes in such a way that a line drawn from the center of the sun to the center of a planet sweeps over equal areas in equal lengths of time.

3. The time it takes a planet to orbit the sun is related to its distance from the sun.

Kepler's laws describe the motion of the planets. They do not explain what causes the planets to move.

Johannes Kepler (1571–1630), a German
astronomer, studied the motion of the planets.

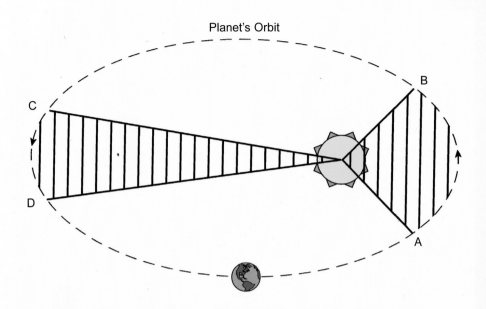

Planet's Orbit

Johannes Kepler discovered from observation that planets orbit the sun in an ellipse, not a perfect circle. Using calculus, Newton was able to prove this fact.

Isaac Newton turned his thoughts to the moon. A moving body keeps on moving in a straight line and at the same speed unless an outside force changes its direction and speed. So why did the moon not shoot off into space? Some outside force must keep it in orbit. The apple falling from a tree provided a key to what that outside force might be. The earth was pulling the moon toward itself. At the same time as the moon was shooting off into space, it was continually being pulled toward the center of the earth.

Newton set out to back up his theory with mathematics. He knew that the pull of gravity grew weaker the farther an object was from the earth. By how much did it grow weaker? He figured that the key to the problem was the inverse-square law. This law states that when the distance between two objects is doubled, the force of gravity between them is one fourth. When the distance is tripled, the force of gravity is one ninth, and so on.

To complete his calculations, Newton needed to know the radius of the earth. The measurement he used was not exact. The answer did not work out as neatly as he had hoped.

Even though the calculation did not work out exactly, Newton was sure he was on the right track. He had satisfied his own need to understand. Almost fifteen years later, he redid the calculation with the correct distance for the earth's radius. Five years after that, he shared his brilliant work with the world.

Meantime, Isaac Newton was busy solving other scientific mysteries.

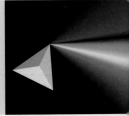

Seeing the Light

ISAAC NEWTON'S DISCOVERIES ABOUT light and color resulted from another purchase he made at Sturbridge Fair; he bought a prism. He already knew that when light passes through a prism it breaks up into the colors of the rainbow. He had also seen fringes of color around objects when he looked through a telescope. The fringe of color made it harder to see an object clearly. He knew that this had something to do with the curved lens in the telescope.

Newton's first experiment with his prism was simple.

By closing the shutters on his window, he could darken his room. He pierced a hole in one shutter so that a beam of sunlight hit the

This display in Grantham Museum shows Newton experimenting with light using a prism.

opposite wall. Here is how he described what he did: "Having darkened my chamber, and made a small hole in my window-shuts, to let in a convenient quantity of the sun's light, I placed my prism . . . [so that the light] might be . . . refracted to the opposite wall."[1]

When the prism was placed in the path of the light beam, the colors of the rainbow showed up on the wall. They were always in the same order—red, orange, yellow, green, blue, indigo, and violet. Could white light really be a mixture of colors? Newton noticed that the colors formed an oblong shape although the hole in the shutter was round. The problem was now a math problem. What made the round beam turn into an oblong shape? The answer must be that the prism refracted (bent) the colors at different angles. It bent the blue light the most and the red light the least.

Newton did another experiment using two prisms. He placed the second prism upside down in front of the first one. The colors came together again to make white light on the back wall. By bringing the colors back together, he had produced white light. The white light was in the shape of a circle.

He tried another experiment. This time, he took a card with a hole in it and placed it between the two prisms, letting only red light pass through the hole. The red light then passed through the second prism. Only red showed on the back wall. He repeated this with the other colors. He was able to isolate each color in turn.

The Great Fire of London

Meantime, London was facing yet another disaster. On the night of September 1, 1666, Samuel Pepys was awakened by his maid, Jane. She told him that the city was on fire. Pepys looked out of the window and then went back to bed. Fires were common in London.

The Lord Mayor was at the scene of the fire. He did not think it was anything to worry about, either. He was against pulling down houses to make a firebreak. This turned out to be a costly mistake. By the next morning, three hundred houses had burned. The wind had risen, and fire was spreading in every direction through the crowded, dirty wooden buildings. The Lord Mayor now wanted houses pulled down everywhere. But the fire was so fierce no one could get close to it.

The Great Fire of London burned for four nights and four days. It destroyed eighty-seven

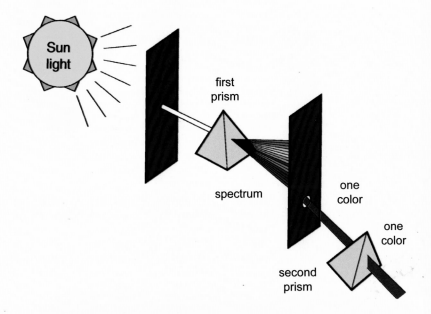

Sun light

first prism

spectrum

one color

one color

second prism

Using a single prism and a pinhole punched in a piece of wood, Newton was able to isolate one color of the spectrum. Sending the same ray of light through a second prism showed that it could not be broken down any further.

churches and over thirteen thousand homes. In time, the city would be rebuilt, but the London of Shakespeare and Queen Elizabeth I was gone. The fire also took care of the problems of rats and filth. The plague was finally over.

Back to Cambridge

Cambridge University opened again in March of the following year. Isaac Newton was studying for his master of arts degree, but it was the fellowship exam in October that would really decide his future. As a fellow, he could continue to live in the university. He could spend the rest of his life as a scholar. Fellows gave lectures and advised students, but there was also plenty of time for reading and studying.

Becoming a fellow was not just based on the results of an exam; politics were involved. Some students had letters of recommendation from the king. It also helped to have friends among the senior fellows who did the choosing. That year, there were nine places to be filled. This was more than usual because no fellowships had been given during the plague years.

When the bell tolled on October 2 to summon the new fellows, Newton was one of the nine. He must have been very relieved. Without a fellowship, he would have had to return to the farm at Woolsthorpe.

Two years after Newton became a fellow, Professor Barrow resigned. He named Isaac Newton to take his place. At the age of twenty-seven, Newton was appointed as professor of mathematics. Few people outside Cambridge knew the brilliant young professor. He still kept most of his ideas to himself.

Newton's Telescope

Isaac Newton continued to be interested in light and color. He wanted to make a telescope that would not have fringes of color around the objects he was looking at. We now know that this can be done by combining lenses of different kinds of glass. Newton chose another way: he used reflecting mirrors instead of lenses. The

Gregory's Idea

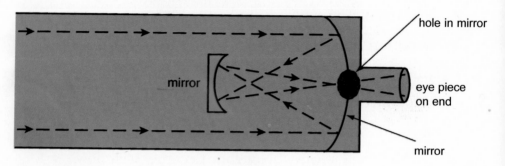

hole in mirror

mirror

eye piece
on end

mirror

Newton's Idea

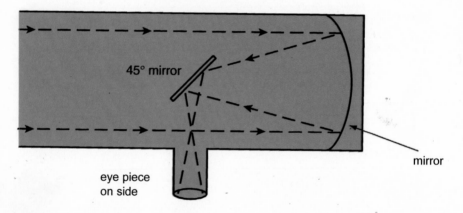

45° mirror

mirror

eye piece
on side

Newton improved on Gregory's idea of using two mirrors
in a telescope. By placing one mirror at an angle,
Newton was able to reflect the light through a side
eyepiece.

idea of using reflecting mirrors was first suggested by James Gregory, a Scottish scientist. However, his plan was not practical. The mirror was placed so that it was in the way of the person looking through the tube. Newton drew a sketch that solved this problem. He placed the mirror at an angle and put a hole for the eyepiece in the side of the tube.

Newton decided to make a telescope to test his idea. His boyhood skill in making models was now being put to good use, but he had a difficult task ahead of him. He had to make everything for himself, even the curved mirrors and lenses. There were no scientific supply catalogs or stores where he could buy what he needed.

The reflecting telescope was a huge success. It was very small, only eight inches long. It gave a clearer and larger image than bigger telescopes of the old type. Newton studied the planets through his telescope. He demonstrated its power to Dr. Barrow.

In 1671, Barrow took the little telescope to

London. He showed it to several important people, including King Charles II, who was anxious to keep up with advances in science. The reflecting telescope was also shown at a meeting of the Royal Society. Everyone was impressed. Henry Oldenberg, the secretary of the society, wrote a description of it. He sent the description to the leading scientists of Europe.

Newton was pleased that his invention caused so much excitement. He was even more pleased when he was invited to become a member of the Royal Society in 1672. At the meeting at which Newton was voted in as a member, a letter was read describing an accurate method for measuring the earth. Newton must not have been aware of this. Otherwise he surely would have reworked his calculations on the orbit of the moon.

The excitement over his telescope drew Newton out of his shell. He decided to share his ideas about light and color. He explained his theories to Oldenberg in a letter that was read aloud at the next meeting of the Royal Society.

A reflecting telescope designed by Newton used a reflecting mirror instead of the usual combination of lenses.

Once again, everyone was impressed. The society decided to publish the letter as a scientific paper, but first the experiments were to be repeated by three members. Two of the people chosen to repeat the experiments were well-known physicists. One was Robert Hooke; the other was Robert Boyle.

Robert Hooke was seven years older than Isaac Newton. The two men had a lot in common. Both had brilliant minds. Both had had difficult, lonely childhoods. Newton outgrew some of his early setbacks. He was now in good health and of average height. Robert Hooke was not so fortunate. He was troubled by sickness all his life. He was very short and had a crooked spine. We have no portrait of him, but Samuel Pepys painted a picture in words. He wrote that Hooke "is the most and promises the least of any man in the world that I ever saw."[2]

Hooke had the right background to judge Newton's experiments. He was interested in how light travels. He had published a paper on the wave theory. Newton's color theory was not based on how light travels, but he mentioned in his letter that he did not lean toward the wave theory. Hooke jumped on this point. Newton's feelings were hurt. He thought it was unfair of Hooke to focus on a side issue.

The quarrel between the two men became heated. Newton said he would never publish anything again. He even said he did not want to belong to the Royal Society. Henry Oldenburg, the secretary, tried to calm Newton down. He wrote to him, saying that the membership "esteems and loves you."[3]

This was not enough to win Newton back. He shut himself away in Cambridge.

5

The Hermit Professor

ISAAC NEWTON STILL SHARED ROOMS IN Trinity College with John Wickins. As a fellow, he now had his own money to spend. His accounts show that he bought a leather carpet for the main room. He built a workbench and bought tools. He and Wickins chose a new couch together.

In spite of living in the middle of a busy university, Newton led a solitary life. He mostly ate in his own room. When he did join the other professors in the college dining room, he was often lost in thought. Sometimes he forgot to eat. If someone asked him a question he usually had a good answer, but he never started a conversation. Nor did he laugh much. A secretary who was with him for five years reported that he only heard Newton laugh once. Newton had lent a friend a copy of Euclid's geometry. The friend asked what good studying Euclid would do. This question made Newton "very merry."[1]

Newton's accounts also show that he spent money on a tablecloth and six napkins, but he did not entertain much. When he did have visitors to his rooms, he was not always a great host. One time he went to his study to get a bottle of wine when a thought came to him. He forgot all about his company. Newton sat down at his desk and lost himself in his work.

Newton was very untidy. He rarely changed his clothes. He did not bother to comb his long hair, which was silvery gray by the time he was thirty years old. Nor did he fasten his shoes. Newton had no hobbies. He did not go out riding, walking, or bowling, or get any other exercise. Any time away from his studies was time lost.

Quite likely, the students and other professors made fun of the eccentric professor,

Many legends surrounding Newton arose after his lifetime. One such legend claimed that he had constructed the Mathematical Bridge that spans the River Cam (above). But it was actually built by James Essex in 1749, twenty-two years after Newton's death.

yet they also respected him. He used to draw diagrams in the gravel of the garden paths. For days afterward, people carefully walked around the sketches.

Although Newton was famous for his brilliant mind, students did not flock to hear his lectures. He was required to give one lecture a week. Very few people attended; sometimes no one was there. Newton's secretary wrote that "few went to hear him, and fewer yet understood him" and that often "for want of hearers, [he] read to the walls."[2]

The Alchemist

After Newton's quarrel with Robert Hooke over his paper on light, he buried himself in his work. He was impatient with any interruption, even letters. He answered one letter saying that he was occupied with some "business of my own which at present [takes up almost all of] my time and thoughts." He ended the letter with the words, "I am in great haste, Yours."[3]

What was keeping Isaac Newton so busy?

It was not mathematics. He now had a new interest; he was spending all his time on chemistry. After reading the works of Robert Boyle, he bought flasks, glass tubes, and chemicals. He built two furnaces in the rooms he shared with John Wickins. Wickins was a very tolerant man. He sometimes even helped Newton with his experiments.

Newton's interest in chemistry led him to a much older subject called alchemy. Alchemy was closely related to chemistry, but it also involved magic and spells. One goal of alchemy was to turn nonprecious metals into gold. However, it was not the search for a way to make gold that interested Newton. He wanted to understand the nature of life itself. He thought that some clue to the nature of life was hidden in the writings of the early alchemists. He spent years making notes from ancient texts, repeating old experiments, and concocting strange medicines.

Newton did not publish any papers on his alchemy experiments. The information we have on these studies comes from his notebooks and loose sheets of paper, which are not easy to read. He kept correcting his notes by writing on top of what he had already written. He sometimes wrote upside down between the lines. He would switch from Latin to English and then back to Latin again. It is hard to tell his own thoughts from notes that he took while reading.

Isaac Newton's papers were left to his heirs.

When they first offered his alchemy notes to Cambridge, the university did not want them. It made people uncomfortable that England's greatest scientist had dabbled in magic. Fifty years later, the notes were accepted. To this day, they make many people uneasy, yet the papers do show the range of the questions that Isaac Newton's great mind explored.

Newton also spent a great deal of time studying the Bible. He was interested in the history of religion. Although he was deeply religious, he did not accept all the beliefs of the Church of England. This almost cost him his career at Cambridge. Every new professor had to become a minister within seven years. By not doing so, Newton would lose his fellowship. Isaac Barrow went to see the king on his friend's behalf. In 1675, Barrow secured an agreement that Newton could be a professor without taking holy orders.

With another crisis behind him, Isaac Newton again buried himself in his studies of alchemy, religion, and mathematics.

6

A Question of Gravity

WHEN ROBERT HOOKE BECAME THE
secretary of the Royal Society in 1678, his job
was to plan meetings. He was also to keep in
touch with members. He sent Isaac Newton a
letter giving him news of the scientific world. He
asked what Newton was doing these days.

Newton wrote back, saying he was involved in
"other business."[1] But he added an experiment
for Hooke to try. The problem was to find the
path of an object falling toward the center of
the earth, taking into account that the earth is
spinning. Newton included a sketch of the
falling object.

When Hooke looked at the sketch, he noticed
an error. He lost no time in pointing it out.
Newton never did like to be told he was wrong,

especially not by Robert Hooke. However, he answered Hooke's letter politely.

This led to more letters from Hooke. In his letters, Hooke suggested that the pull of gravity between two large objects is not constant. Its strength decreases in proportion to the distance between the objects.

Although Newton ignored Hooke's letters, they did remind him of his earlier calculations on the orbit of the moon. By this time he knew that he had not been using the correct distance for the radius of the earth. He redid his calculations. Even before he was finished, he could tell that he could explain the moon's orbit around the earth. He became so excited that his hand shook too much to complete the arithmetic. He had to have someone else do it for him.

Even though Newton was excited about his results, he did not rush out and tell everyone. Instead, he shoved the calculations into a drawer.

Family Concerns

The following May, sadness touched Isaac Newton's life. His mother had a fever and was very ill. The family sent for Newton, who came home and stayed at his mother's bedside until her death. He "sate up whole nights with her, gave her all her Physick himself, and dressed all her blisters with his own hands . . ."[2]

Isaac Newton then had the sad duty of arranging for his mother's funeral. She was buried in the Colsterworth churchyard beside his father. In her will she left small sums of money to her other children, Mary, Hannah, and Benjamin. Most of her property, including Woolsthorpe Manor, went to Isaac.

Some of the land was rented out. One of Newton's tenants was Edward Storer, with whom he had lived while he attended school in Grantham. Storer turned out to be a troublesome tenant. He was always behind in the rent, and he ignored Newton's letters. Eight years later, Newton was still having problems

Hannah Newton Smith was buried in Colsterworth churchyard in 1679.

with Storer, who had neglected the buildings and fences, and had not paid his rent.

Newton was on good terms with Edward's brother, Arthur, who must have forgotten their playground fight. Arthur had left England and now lived in Maryland Colony. He was interested in astronomy. He and Newton wrote each other letters about the stars.

The London Coffeehouse Meeting

In 1684, a conversation in a London coffeehouse had a big effect on Isaac Newton's career. Robert Hooke was talking about the movement of the planets with his friends Christopher Wren and Edmund Halley. They agreed with the German astronomer Johannes Kepler that planets travel in an ellipse. But could this be proved mathematically?

Christopher Wren offered to give a prize to anyone who could produce the proof within two months. The prize was to be a book worth forty shillings. The proof would be recorded and published. Hooke said he could provide the

Christopher Wren (1632–1723) was a founding member of the Royal Society.

Edmund Halley (1656–1742) said that the orbit of a comet is an ellipse. He correctly predicted when the comet of 1682 would return, and the comet is now called Halley's comet.

answer, but he would not tell them yet. He wanted to give Halley time to try, so that he would realize how difficult the problem was.

Halley gave the problem some thought, but he was sure he could not win the prize. Two months passed, and Hooke did not claim the prize either. Halley was disappointed. Having proof that the inverse-square law applied to the planets would help him with his observations in astronomy. He decided that there was only one person who could solve the problem and that was Isaac Newton. He told Wren he was going to visit the hermit scientist.

Without wasting any more time, Halley set off for Cambridge. He went straight to Newton's rooms and asked about the path of a planet. Newton answered that it was an ellipse. When Halley then asked him how he could be so sure, Newton calmly said he had already proved it mathematically.

He could not, however, find the important calculation. It was now several years since he had shoved it into a drawer. He promised to rework the problem and send it to Halley in London.

In November 1684, Halley received the proof he had been waiting for. It came in the form of a nine-page paper written in Latin. In his hands, Halley held the answer to the question of why planets travel around the sun in an ellipse. He was overawed by Isaac Newton. Newton had made a tremendously important discovery, but he had not bothered to tell anyone about it.

We owe Edmund Halley a great debt. If he had not made that trip to Cambridge, it is hard to say how long Newton's results would have stayed hidden.

The *Principia*

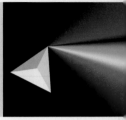

ISAAC NEWTON'S SHORT PAPER ON THE
movement of the planets seemed to trigger the
creative forces in his great brain. His mind again
became totally focused on mathematics, and he
decided to expand the paper into a book. Soon
Newton's life was taken over by his writing.
Meals were not important; he mostly snacked on
bread and water. He never sat down at the
dining table. Nor did he go to bed at night; he
took short naps without undressing. He became
sloppier than ever. However, that did not matter
much, because he rarely left his rooms. The only
thing that he cared about was getting his
thoughts onto paper. He was exact and logical in
doing that.

Gravity Again

Newton returned to the questions that had interested him as he sat under the apple tree in the garden at Woolsthorpe. Gravity pulled on an apple falling toward the earth. It pulled on the planets as they journeyed around the sun. It pulled on a bullet fired from a gun.

Newton's mind took another giant leap forward. Not only did the earth pull on the apple; the apple also pulled on the earth. The amount of pull depended on the object's mass. (Mass is the amount of matter in an object.) This led to Newton's universal law of gravitation: Every particle in the universe is attracted to every other particle. The force of their attraction is related to their masses and their distance apart from each

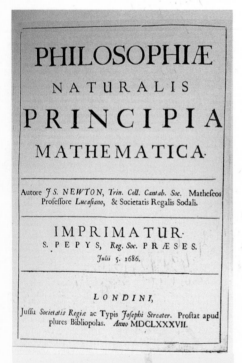

The title page of the *Principia*.

other. All the motion in the solar system obeys the same law.

Newton needed data to prove his law. He wrote to John Flamsteed, the Astronomer Royal. Flamsteed sent him figures on the position of stars and on the orbits of the planets.

Mathematical Principles of Natural Philosophy is the English title of Newton's book. (Natural philosophy is now called physics.) It is mostly known as the *Principia*. He wrote it in Latin in three volumes. Newton finished the first volume before Easter of 1685, and the second volume was completed by late summer. He spent several months revising them and then sent them to Halley at the Royal Society.

The society had just published a big, expensive book called *A History of Fishes*. There was not enough money in the budget to publish the *Principia*. Halley offered to put up his own money to publish it although he was not a wealthy man. His father had just died without leaving a will. Until the estate was settled, he depended on the Royal Society for his income.

But the society was so short of money that he had been paid with just fifty copies of *Fishes*. In spite of all his money problems, Halley made the arrangements to publish Newton's book. He acted as editor and carefully checked all the diagrams.

At this point, Newton and Robert Hooke got into another quarrel. Hooke claimed he had been first to come up with the inverse-square law that was part of the proof. Even if he had, he had not done the mathematics to prove the law. No one except Newton took Hooke's claim seriously. Newton, however, became very upset and said he would not finish the third volume.

Halley was stunned. Without volume three, the first two volumes were not likely to sell. Halley would end up seriously in debt. But that was not his main concern. He did not want the great work to be incomplete. Halley wrote Newton a tactful letter. Newton agreed to go back to work.

Published at Last

The *Principia* came out on July 5, 1687, as a Royal Society publication. Samuel Pepys was president of the society at this time, and his name is on the cover above the date. The nine-page letter that Newton had written in answer to Halley's question had grown to 511 pages. Bound in leather, the book sold for nine shillings.

The book was not easy to read, but it sold well. People realized that it was a very important work. Because the *Principia* was written in Latin, which was the language of science, scholars in other countries were able to read it. It was eventually translated into many different languages. The first English translation came out in 1729, two years after Newton's death. It was done by Andrew Motte.

A new translation by I. Bernard Cohen and Anne Whitman was published in 1999.[1] Like the original, it is not "an easy read." It contains 974 pages. The first eleven chapters are a reader's guide to Newton's *Principia*. Chapter Ten is called "How to Read the *Principia*." It includes five pages of other books that would help the reader understand Newton's great work.

The Laws of Motion

The *Principia* contains Newton's three laws of motion. These laws are the foundation of the science of mechanics. They apply both to simple machines and to rockets that send spaceships into orbit and off to the planets.

Newton's three laws of motion state:

1. Every object stays at rest unless it is acted on by an outside force. If it is in motion, it travels in a straight line unless it is acted on by an outside force.

2. The outside force is related to the direction and the increase speed of the object.

3. To every action there is an opposite and equal reaction.

In volume three of the *Principia*, Newton showed how his theory applied to moons, planets, and comets. He explained the earth's tides. He said that because the earth spins, it is not completely round; it is flattened at the poles. An expedition to Lapland proved this to be true nine years after Newton's death.

The Comet's Return

Halley was excited about Newton's observations on comets. If, as Newton stated, the orbit of a comet is an ellipse, then the same comet should be seen from the earth at regular intervals. A very bright comet had appeared in 1682. Halley began to search old records to find when bright comets had been seen in the past. He worked on the problem for over twenty years. He knew that Johannes Kepler had described a bright comet in 1607. In old manuscripts, he found that comets had appeared in 1531 and before that in 1456. He decided that the same comet was showing up at seventy-six-year intervals. He predicted that the 1682 comet would return in 1758. He did not live to see it, but when it was seen in 1758, the comet was named after him. In

Law I

Law II

Law III

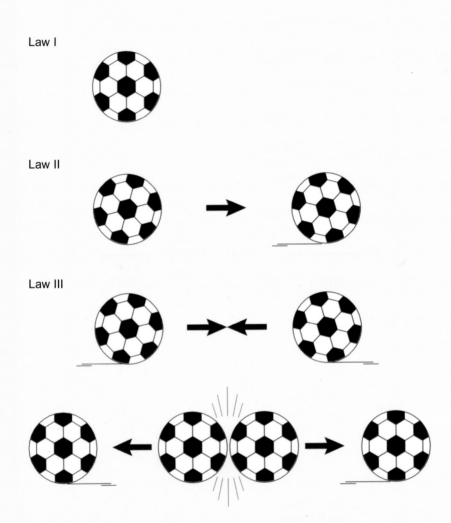

Using soccer balls can help explain Newton's laws of motion. Law I shows that if no force acts on the soccer ball, it will not move. Law II shows that the ball will move when a force acts upon it. In the case of Law III, if two balls are pushed toward each other, they will bounce off one another and travel in the opposite direction. That is, there will be an opposite reaction.

this century, Halley's Comet will not appear until 2062.

Charles II died two years before the *Principia* was published. Although he might not have understood it, he would have been impressed. A copy was presented to his brother James II, who was now king. James, however, was not interested in science. The king was not the only person unexcited about the *Principia*. While Newton was walking through Trinity College, one of his students pointed to him and said, "There goes the man that writt a book that neither he nor any body else understands."[2]

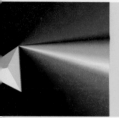

8

Outside Forces

UNTIL HE WAS FORTY-FIVE, ISAAC NEWTON'S life followed a straight line. The "sober, silent, thinking lad" became a sober, silent, thinking man. Then, with the *Principia* almost finished, his life took off in a new direction. The outside force that caused this change in direction was the king of England himself.

King James II wrote to John Peachell at Cambridge, asking him to award a master of arts degree to Father Albin Francis, a monk. Francis would not have to "performe the Exercises" or take "any Oath or Oaths whatsoever."[1]

Some of the university officials wanted to fulfill the king's request. They thought they should bend the rules this one time. Isaac Newton disagreed. He said that if King James were allowed to get involved in university affairs, there was no saying where it would end. Newton convinced the officials not to do the king's bidding.

When James heard that the university would not do as he asked, he ordered John Peachell to appear in court. Judge Jeffreys, who was to hear the case, was known as a "hanging judge." He was both brutal and unfair.

The university chose eight professors to accompany Peachell. Newton was one of them. Jeffreys could tell that Peachell was timid and ill prepared. He aimed all his remarks at Peachell, who became so nervous that he could not put up a good defense. The judge found Peachell guilty of disobedience and stripped him of his job. The other professors, who never got the chance to speak, got off lightly. Jeffreys dismissed them with a threat. He told them, "Go your way, and sin no more, lest a worse thing come unto you."[2]

Politics

In the end, Albin Francis did not get his master's degree and James II did nothing about it. By this time, he had troubles of his own. In the

KING WILLIAM AT THE BATTLE OF THE BOYNE.

William of Orange (on the white horse) and his wife Mary, daughter of James II, were invited by Parliament to take over the throne of England in 1688. Since then, every ruler of England has been a Protestant.

summer of 1688, his second wife gave birth to a son. James already had a grown-up daughter, Mary. She was a Protestant and was married to Prince William in Holland. Until the baby boy was born, she had been next in line to the throne. Some English people were not happy that there was now a new heir who would be brought up as a Catholic.

In November, William came over from Holland with six hundred ships to invade England. James II fled to France. Most people were glad to see him go. They called William's

The modern Houses of Parliament in London were completed in 1867. When Isaac Newton was a member of Parliament, meetings were held in St. Stephen's Chapel in Westminster Palace. The palace was destroyed by fire in 1834, but the chapel survived and can still be seen today.

takeover the Glorious Revolution because no blood was shed. People had been afraid of another civil war.

After Newton's success in university affairs, he got into national politics. He ran for Parliament. In 1689, he was elected to represent the university. He was a member of Parliament for only one year, but it turned out to be an important year. He took part in the vote that proclaimed William and Mary to be king and queen of England. He voted on the Bill of Rights, which limited the power of the king and gave more rights to citizens. The Bill of Rights became the model for the first ten amendments of the Constitution of the United States. The Toleration Act, which was passed while Newton was a member, granted English people more religious freedom than they had before. Although Newton voted for these new laws, he did not take part in the debates. In fact, there is only one record of him saying anything all year—when he asked an usher to close the window!

Newton's Black Year

In the fall of 1693, Isaac Newton had severe health problems. He suffered a mental breakdown. He sent strange letters to friends, accusing them of plotting against him.

In a letter to Samuel Pepys, he wrote, "I must withdraw from your acquaintance, and see neither you nor the rest of my friends any more."[3] Pepys was worried when he read the letter. He asked a friend in Cambridge to check up on Newton. Newton told this friend that he remembered sending the letter although he now had no idea what was in it. He had written it after not sleeping for five nights in a row.

News of Isaac Newton's breakdown spread all through Europe. Some said it was caused by his losing some of his papers in a fire. (This often happened when people wrote by candlelight.) Others said that Newton was paying the price for years of overwork.

A recent theory is that he may have been suffering from mercury poisoning. He used mercury, then called quicksilver, in his chemistry and alchemy experiments. Some of the symptoms of mercury poisoning are loss of memory and not being able to sleep or eat. Bleeding gums and loose teeth are also symptoms. Newton did not have any of these symptoms, however; he had healthy teeth.

Newton himself joked about the effect of mercury. His hair was silvery gray by the time he was thirty years old. When John Wickins claimed that his friend's hair was gray because he worked so hard, Newton said it was because of "the Experiments he made so often with Quick Silver."[4]

We probably never will know what caused Newton's Black Year. Mental illness is often hard to explain. It is almost impossible to explain an illness that took place three hundred years ago.

By 1696, Newton was completely well. He was ready to take on new challenges. His life took off in yet another direction. This time the outside force was the offer of a job; Isaac Newton was asked to be Warden of the Mint.

9

The Mint

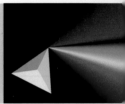

WHEN NEWTON BECAME WARDEN OF THE Mint in 1696, he moved to London. The city would be his home for the next thirty years. During his long life, Newton did very little traveling. Lincolnshire, Cambridge, and London were the only places he knew. But that did not limit his journeys of the mind.

The letter that offered Newton the job as warden stated that "[it] has not too much bus'ness to require more attendance than you may spare. . . ."[1] In other words, he would not need to work very hard. The person who ran the Mint was called the Master of the Mint. The warden did not have to make decisions. Newton, however, was not someone who did things by halves. He always took work seriously.

New Coins for Old

When Newton joined the staff of the Mint, the coin system in England was in a state of crisis. Before 1660, when Charles II became king, coins were made by hand. Handmade coins were not completely round, and the faces on the coins often were off center. Because the coins were not uniform, it was easy for people to counterfeit them. Counterfeit (fake) coins were almost as plentiful as real ones. Another common way of cheating was to clip or shave the edges of silver coins. With its edges clipped, a coin still looked much the same and could be used. The clippings and shavings could be melted down and sold as pure silver.

Making coins by machine was supposed to solve these problems. Machine-made coins had marked or milled edges. This would put the clippers out of business. It would be easy to see if a coin had been clipped. But the new coins presented another problem. The silver they contained was worth more than the value of the coin itself. People melted them down, and new

The Mint was located in the Tower of London when Isaac Newton was warden.

coins disappeared almost as soon as they were minted. Meanwhile, people still squabbled over the old clipped and counterfeit coins. Everyone was eager to spend them, but no one wanted to accept them.

Shortly before Newton became the warden, Parliament voted to call in all the old coins. The Mint would make new ones to replace the old ones. It was a big job. It was also an expensive job. Workers at the Mint had to work overtime to make the new money. The early shift started at 4:00 a.m., and the last shift ended at midnight.

The recoinage was paid for out of a new tax that was based on the number of windows in each house. Owners of big houses with lots of windows paid higher taxes. To reduce their taxes, some people sealed up windows. This happened at Woolsthorpe Manor. One of the windows in Newton's old room was blocked off. His carvings on the windowsill were covered over. They came to light years later when the window was unblocked.

The Mint was located between the outer and the inner walls of the Tower of London. The buildings included workshops, stores, stables, and the warden's house. The warden's house faced a high wall. It was gloomy and noisy—and it smelled bad! A lot of the machinery at the Mint was turned by horses. The annual bill for disposing of horse manure was seven hundred pounds.

The House on Jermyn Street

After a few weeks, Newton decided to move. He bought a house on Jermyn Street and set about furnishing it. He chose red drapes, a red couch, and red hangings. He invited his niece, Catherine Barton, to be his hostess and housekeeper. Catherine was the daughter of his half-sister Hannah. She was a witty and beautiful young woman.

Isaac Newton became very fond of Catherine. A letter written to her when she was ill shows his concern. A year or two after she moved to London, Catherine caught smallpox. She was away visiting friends in the country at the time. Newton wrote, "Pray let me know by the next how your face is, and if the fever be going. Perhaps warm milk from the cow may help to abate it. I am your very loving uncle, Is. Newton."[2]

Catherine recovered completely.

Newton entertained more in London than he did in Cambridge, but he still liked to live quietly. He did not often attend concerts or the theater; he spent most of his spare time reading and studying. After attending the opera, he said, "The first act gave me the greatest pleasure. The second quite tired me: at the third I ran away."[3]

Meantime, things were going well at the Mint. Newton had the right skills for the job. He was good at problem solving; and he had no trouble mastering the accounting system. From his studies in alchemy, he knew about the nature of metal. He also knew how to combine metals to make alloys.

In 1700, Isaac Newton became Master of the Mint. He was now head of the whole operation. Never before had a warden been promoted to master.

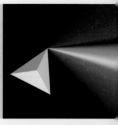

10

"The Great Ocean of Truth"

WHEN ISAAC NEWTON FIRST MOVED TO London, he was very busy at the Mint. He did not attend meetings of the Royal Society. The programs at the meetings at that time were quite dull. Besides, Robert Hooke would have been there. Newton still did not get along with him. After Hooke died in March 1703, Newton became active in the society. He was elected president that same year. His fame attracted new members and revived an interest in science.

With the Mint running smoothly, Newton now had time for his own work. In 1704, he published a book, *Opticks*, that contained his early experiments on light and color. He also revised the *Principia*. For his new edition, Newton needed more records on the position of

John Flamsteed (1646–1719) used his telescope to observe the positions of the stars and the orbits of the planets.

the moon. John Flamsteed, who had helped him earlier, sent him the information. When Flamsteed found some mistakes in the figures he had sent, he sent new figures. Newton grew annoyed when the figures kept changing. Flamsteed was not happy either; he wanted to know what Newton was doing with the data. He resented Newton's impatience and the way he demanded more and more information. This led to a quarrel between the two men that went on for years.

Old Enemies

Meantime, Newton was still arguing with Wilhelm Leibniz over who deserved the credit for inventing calculus. One of Leibniz's friends sent Newton a mathematical problem. Scientists often exchange puzzles and problems, but the friend may have been hoping to stump Newton. Then he could say that Newton was not as sharp as he used to be.

The problem was waiting for Newton when he came home at four o'clock in the afternoon. He was tired after a hard day at the Mint. Nevertheless, he went straight to work on the problem. He worked through the night and had it solved by four in the morning. He sent his calculations back without signing his name, but Leibniz's friend knew who had come up with the answer. He said, "The lion is recognized from its print."[1]

In 1705, Isaac was greatly honored when Queen Anne made him a knight. The event took place at Trinity College in Cambridge. The farm lad from Lincolnshire had come a long way. He was now Sir Isaac Newton.

New Friends

Newton's biographer William Stukeley, who was also from Lincolnshire, was a student at Cambridge at this time. He went on to become a doctor in London and joined the Royal Society. There he met his hero, Isaac Newton, who invited Stukeley to his home. The two men became friends. Newton enjoyed talking about his old school days in Grantham. Without Stukeley's biography, we would not know much about Newton's childhood.

John Conduitt was another young man who was close to Newton in his old age. Conduitt married Newton's niece, Catherine, in 1717. He collected stories about his famous uncle-in-law and kept notes on all their conversations.

Newton enjoyed good health until near the end of his long life. He looked young for a man in his eighties. His white hair remained thick. He had strong teeth and keen eyesight. A few days before his death, the rector (priest) visited him. Afterward, the rector wrote that he found Newton writing "without the help of spectacles, at the greatest distance of the room from the windows, and with a parcel of books on the table, casting a shade upon the paper. Seeing this . . . I said to him, 'Sir, you seem to be writing in a place where you cannot so well see.' His answer was, 'A little light serves me.'"[2]

In January 1725, Isaac Newton came down with a bad cough. Catherine thought it was caused by the smoky air in London. She persuaded her uncle to move out to Kensington. The air was fresher in the country. Today, Kensington is in the middle of London.

Newton still went to meetings of the Royal Society, though not regularly. The last meeting

Isaac Newton's statue stands in Trinity College, Cambridge.

he attended was on March 2, 1727. By the time he got back to Kensington two days later, he was very ill. He died on March 20 at the age of eighty-four.

The minutes of the Royal Society for March 23 read, "The Chair being Vacant by the Death of Sir Isaac Newton there was no Meeting this Day."[3]

Isaac Newton was honored in death, as he had been in life. He was buried in Westminster Abbey, where a huge monument was erected in his memory. The text on the monument reads, "Let Mortals rejoice that there has existed so great an Ornament to the Human Race."

Isaac Newton summed up his own life more simply. Shortly before he died, he told a friend, "I don't know what I may seem to the world, but, as to myself, I seem to have been only like a boy playing on the sea shore, and diverting myself in now and then finding a smoother pebble or a prettier shell than ordinary, [while] the great ocean of truth lay all undiscovered before me."[4]

"On the Shoulders of Giants"

ISAAC NEWTON LIVED AT THE RIGHT time. He was able to take advantage of the great advances that were taking place in the field of science. However, those early physicists and astronomers were not known as scientists. They were natural philosophers. The word scientist did not come into use until the mid-eighteen hundreds.

For nearly two hundred years, scholars had been questioning old beliefs and coming up with new ideas. One of those groundbreaking astronomers was a Polish monk named Nicolaus Copernicus (1473–1543). As a young man, Copernicus was an avid reader. He was fortunate to be able to read books by ancient Greek thinkers, such as Aristotle and Ptolemy.

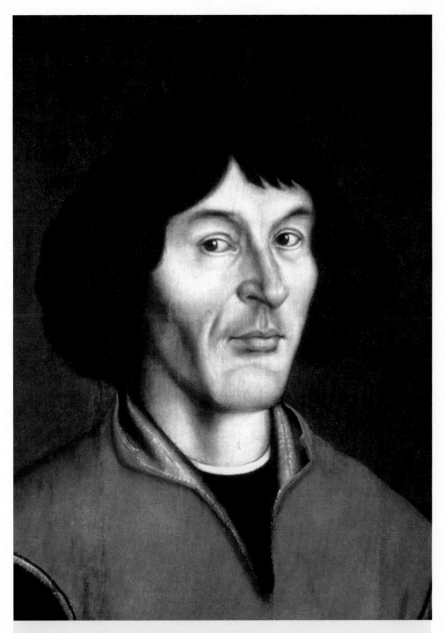

Nicolaus Copernicus (1473–1543) did not believe the earth was the center of the universe, but rather that the stars and planets revolved around the sun.

Just twenty years before Copernicus was born, Johannes Gutenberg had invented the printing press. Now that books did not have to be copied by hand, they were easier to come by.

Copernicus did not agree with everything he read. He questioned the statement that the earth does not move, and that the sun, stars, and planets all circle around it. Instead, he proposed that the planets and the earth travel around the sun in circles. This was a bold idea that most people did not want to hear. They preferred to go on thinking that the earth was the center of the universe.

Johannes Kepler (1571–1630) followed up on the work of Copernicus. He agreed that the planets orbit the sun. But he did not think they moved in perfect circles. He said that each planet travels in a flattened oval orbit called an ellipse. He also said that the speed of a planet varies with its distance from the sun.

Galileo (1564–1642) was another scientist who questioned long-held beliefs. He was one of the first people to understand the importance

Galileo Galilei (1564–1642) discovered several laws of motion by conducting experiments.

of trying to prove a theory by doing experiments. One of his experiments challenged a question that went back to the time of Aristotle: If two different objects are dropped from the same height, does the heavier one hit the ground first? Galileo designed an experiment to find out. He dropped several weights from the Leaning Tower of Pisa. They fell at the same speed. He also noticed that the speed of a falling object increases with the length of time it falls.

Galileo's studies of motion later helped Newton develop the law of gravity. Although Newton worked alone, he was well aware of the debt he owed earlier scientists. When he was an old man, he was asked how he came up with so many new ideas. He answered, "If I have seen further [than most men], it is by standing on the shoulders of giants."[1] Some of these giants were Copernicus, Kepler, and Galileo.

Building on Newton's Ideas

The centuries after Isaac Newton are full of giants who have stood on Newton's shoulders.

Michael Faraday, a famous nineteenth-century scientist, saw electricity and magnetism as being linked together as a force in the universe, like gravity. Faraday had an unusual background for a great scientist. He was born into a poor family. He never attended a high school or a university. When he was thirteen, he went to work for a bookbinder. It turned out to be the right place for a youth who was interested in science. He learned a lot about electricity by reading about it in the *Encyclopaedia Britannica*. He spent many hours taking notes from chemistry textbooks.

When Faraday was twenty-two, he was offered a job as a laboratory assistant. He now had more chances to do experiments. He produced new chemical compounds and added to the knowledge of how elements combine. His greatest claim to fame is in the field of electricty and magnetism. He discovered that moving a magnet in and out of a coil of wire produces an electric current in the wire.

Unlike Newton, Faraday did not know enough mathematics to back up his theories.

That was left to the brilliant mathematician James Clerk Maxwell. While he was at Cambridge University, Maxwell became interested in Faraday's work on electricity and magnetism. Some years later, he came up with four mathematical formulas that show that Faraday's ideas about electromagnetism were correct. The formulas are known as "Maxwell's equations."

Maxwell's equations are able to predict the speed of light. His work eventually led to the discovery of radio waves, X rays, and other invisible rays. It laid the foundation for the electrically powered world we live in today.

The Problem With Time

Albert Einstein was born in Germany in 1879, the year that James Maxwell died. When he was a small boy, his father gave him a compass. Young Albert's mind was full of questions. What is magnetism? What makes the compass needle point to the north?

Twenty years later, Einstein was still

fascinated by magnetism and electricity. He worked in the Swiss National Patent Office in Bern. His job involved writing reports on new inventions. He found this interesting, but he also made time for working on his own ideas and theories.

In 1905, Einstein, like Newton, had a "miracle year." He wrote five brilliant scientific papers in six months. His ideas once again challenged people's view of the world. One of his papers changed the way scientists think about time, distance, and speed. Newton believed that time is always the same. It might not be the same on every clock, but a minute is always a minute and an hour is always an hour no matter where you are. Newton said, "Absolute, true, and mathematical time, in and of itself and of its own nature, without reference to anything external, flows uniformly and by another name is called duration."[2] Concerning space, he wrote, "Absolute space, of its own nature without reference to anything external, always remains homogeneous [the same

Albert Einstein (1879–1955) is famous for his theory of relativity, which focused on time, space, mass, motion, and gravitation.

throughout] and immovable."[3] Einstein's new idea about time applied to the entire universe. He said that the rate at which time flows depends on where you are and how fast you are traveling. In other words, time is not absolute.

Einstein also looked at gravity in a new way. He often reached his conclusions by simply using his imagination. He did "thought experiments." One day, while sitting in the patent office, he pictured a housepainter falling from the roof of a building. Although the painter keeps falling faster and faster, he feels as if he is floating. He does not feel the pull of gravity. From this image, Einstein reasoned that gravity and acceleration are equivalent.

Thought Experiments

Try this thought experiment about the law of gravity. Imagine you are in a spaceship with no windows. The spaceship is sitting on the earth's surface. If you drop an apple, it falls to the floor. Newton would have said that gravity pulled the apple downward. Now you are shooting off into space beyond the earth's gravity. The spaceship is accelerating. What happens when you let go of the apple? The floor of the speeding spaceship moves upward toward it. But because there are no windows in the spaceship, the apple seems to you to be falling. You cannot tell the pull of gravity from the force of acceleration. As Einstein puts it, they are equivalent.

Here is another thought experiment without any right answer. Imagine that in 1705—the year when Isaac Newton became Sir Isaac Newton—Newton jumps foward two hundred years in time. And suppose he has bridged the space between Cambridge, England, and the patent office in Bern, Switzerland. What would he and Einstein have had to say to one another?

The two men would have a lot to talk about. They had much in common. They were both young when they had their "miracle years," and they both had a great ability to give their entire mind to any problem that interested them. But Newton might not have been too pleased to learn that Albert Einstein was questioning his law of gravity! Newton was very thin-skinned when it came to criticism. He never did forgive Robert Hooke for disagreeing with him. On the other hand, Newton was always looking for a greater understanding of the universe.

Now let us jump Newton forward another hundred years. He lands in *your* living room.

The great man of science asks, "What's new in the universe?"

What do you tell him?

Activities

The key to Isaac Newton's genius was his power of thought. He once explained that when he was faced with a problem he kept it in his mind until he solved it. He often went without food or sleep until he was satisfied with his answer. Few people in the history of the world have been gifted with such powers of concentration.

In this chapter, you will find a few experiments to challenge your mind. In some, you are left to find the answer for yourself. Your parents may not let you skip meals and stay up late until you are satisfied with your answers. They may not think that you are a genius at work—but Isaac Newton's mother did not appreciate that her child was a genius, either!

Newton's Rings—The Color of Light

Sometimes you can see the colors of the rainbow in an oily puddle. These rings of color are known as Newton's Rings. You can also see them in a soap bubble.

Newton used a prism he bought at Sturbridge Fair to break up light into separate colors. You can do this same experiment with a baking pan and a small mirror.

Materials

- a baking pan
- a small rectangular mirror
- a white sheet of paper
- an index card with a pinhole in it

Procedure

1. Fill the pan with water.

2. Lean a mirror against the edge of the pan with its lower half in the water.

3. Place the pan so that the sun shines on the mirror.

4. On a white sheet of paper, catch the rainbow of light that is reflected from the mirror.

5. You can isolate the colors, just as Newton did, by holding the index card an inch or two in front of the white paper and moving it up and down

so that a pinpoint of red, yellow, or blue light passes through the hole and shines on the paper.

To see the colors on soap bubbles, add a little sugar to a detergent or soap bubble solution. This lets you blow bigger bubbles. How does the size of the bubble affect the brightness of the color?

Where else can you see rainbows? What makes a double rainbow?

The Inverse-Square Law

The pull of gravity between two objects becomes less as the distance between them increases. So does the brightness of a light. The farther you move from a light, the dimmer it appears. When the distance between you and the source of light is doubled, the light appears only one fourth as bright. It follows the inverse-square law—the same law that Hooke, Wren, and Halley discussed in a London coffee shop in 1684.

You can demonstrate the inverse-square law with a Mini Maglite® flashlight—a flashlight that gives off a point of light.

Materials

- a Mini Maglite® flashlight with the reflector unscrewed
- an index card
- graph paper with 1/2-inch or 1/4-inch squares

Procedure

1. Cut a 1/2-inch by 1/2-inch square hole in the middle of the index card.

2. Paste the graph paper onto a piece of cardboard to make it easier to position.

3. Hold or fix the index card one inch from the light source so that a square of light shines onto the graph paper.

4. Keeping the index card one inch from the light, move the graph paper farther away. As you move the graph paper, the number of squares that are lit up increases.

To demonstrate the inverse-square law, first place the graph paper against the index card. A single 1/2-inch square is lit up. Move the graph paper one inch away from the card. It is now two inches from the source of light. How many squares are lit up? Now move the graph paper another inch away, so that it is three inches from the light. Record your results each time you move the graph paper. What happens to the brightness of the light as it spreads over a larger area of the paper?

Using Your Marbles

Challenge your friends to move a marble from one paper cup to another without touching either the marble or the cups. Then show them that it can be done with the help of the force of gravity.

Materials

- a marble
- two 5-ounce paper cups
- masking tape
- a yardstick

Procedure

1. Cut one cup down so that the sides are about one inch tall.

2. Tape this cup to one end of the yardstick and place the marble in it.

3. Tape the taller cup about 4 inches along the yardstick from the first.

4. Tape the other end of the yardstick to the door frame at floor level. The tape forms a hinge so that the stick can be raised.

5. Raise the end of the yardstick until it is about 20 inches above the floor.

6. You are now ready to move the marble without touching either cup.

7. Release the yardstick with a light downward push.

The marble should fall into the other cup. How does this come about? The marble falls in a straight line under the force of gravity. The cups follow a curved path, as is shown in the diagram. It may take a little practice to push down with the exact force so that the marble lands in the other cup. If the marble falls short

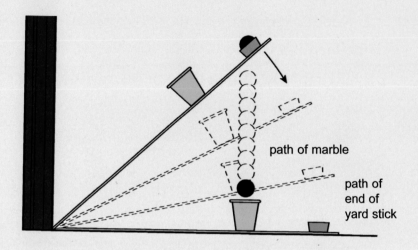

path of marble

path of
end of
yard stick

of the cup, give a stronger push. If it goes too far,
push down less hard.

Defying Gravity

Here is a demonstration that seems to go against
the law of gravity.

Materials

- two cones or funnels
- masking tape
- two sticks or dowels
- two books of different sizes

Procedure

1. Join the flat surfaces of the cones or funnels with tape.

2. Stand the books on their sides.

3. Place the sticks across the two books so that they are farther apart on the taller book (see diagram).

4. Place the double cone at the bottom of the slope.

The cones roll uphill! What is going on?

Although the cones seem to be moving upward, their center of gravity is actually moving

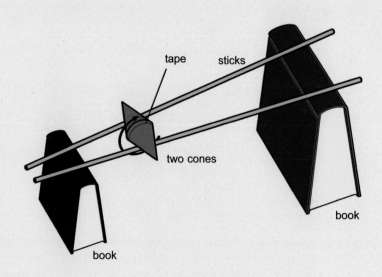

Isaac Newton: The Greatest Scientist of All Time

downward. A body's center of gravity is the point around which its weight is balanced. The cones are really sinking lower between the sticks.

The Age of Miracles

We live in an age of miracles beyond anything Isaac Newton dreamed of. Take a look around you at all the things that would baffle the great mind of science. When Newton studied optics, he never guessed that surgeons would someday use laser beams of light to do operations. Newton spent years thinking about magic and alchemy. The alchemist's goal was to change other metals into gold. Nuclear scientists can now do this, though it is too costly to be worth it.

Isaac Newton's genius was not just based on answering questions. It was based on asking them. If he were alive today, Newton would approach science in the same way as he did three hundred years ago. He would not take any of the miracles that surround us for granted.

Chronology

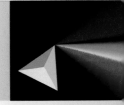

1642—Isaac Newton, the elder, dies in October. Isaac Newton is born at Woolsthorpe Manor on December 25.

1642–1646—English Civil War.

1646—Hannah Newton marries Barnabas Smith.

1649—Charles I is beheaded.

1653—Oliver Cromwell becomes Lord Protector of England.

1655—Isaac starts grammar school in Grantham.

1660—The Restoration: The monarchy is restored and Charles II becomes king.

1661—Isaac enters Trinity College, Cambridge.

1664—The plague breaks out in London.

1665–1666—Isaac Newton's "miracle years."

1666—The Great Fire of London.

1667—Newton is made a fellow at Trinity College.

1669—Newton is appointed professor of mathematics.

1672—Newton is made a member of the Royal Society.

1679—Hannah Newton Smith dies.

1684—Newton returns to the study of gravity.

1687—Publication of the *Principia*.

1688—The Glorious Revolution. James II flees England and William III and Mary II become joint rulers.

1689—Newton becomes a member of Parliament.

1693—Newton suffers a mental breakdown.

1696—Newton moves to London as Warden of the Mint.

1700—Newton is appointed Master of the Mint.

1703—Newton becomes president of the Royal Society.

1704—Publication of *Opticks*.

1705—Newton is knighted by Queen Anne.

1727—Newton dies on March 20.

Chapter Notes

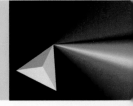

Chapter 1. "A Sober, Silent, Thinking Lad"

1. Gale E. Christianson, *In the Presence of the Creator* (New York: The Free Press, 1984), p. 4.

2. William Stukeley, *Memoirs of Sir Isaac Newton's Life* (London: Taylor and Francis, 1936), pp. 45–46.

3. Ibid., p. 46.

4. Ibid.

5. Ibid., p. 42.

6. Ibid., p. 41.

7. Ibid., p. 39.

Chapter 2. New Horizons

1. William Stukeley, *Memoirs of Sir Isaac Newton's Life* (London: Taylor and Francis, 1936), p. 51.

2. Richard S. Westfall, *Never at Rest* (Cambridge, England: Cambridge University Press, 1980), p. 74. John Wickins's son wrote this in a letter to a friend many years later.

3. Ibid., p. 104.

4. Stukeley, p. 53.

Chapter 3. A Fruitful Vacation

1. Richard S. Westfall, *Never at Rest* (Cambridge, England: Cambridge University Press, 1980), p. 143.

2. William Stukeley, *Memoirs of Sir Isaac Newton's Life* (London: Taylor and Francis, 1936), p. 20.

Chapter 4. Seeing the Light

1. Gale E. Christianson, *In the Presence of the Creator* (New York: The Free Press, 1984), p. 92.

2. Ibid., p. 157.

3. Ibid., p. 180.

Chapter 5. The Hermit Professor

1. William Stukeley, *Memoirs of Sir Isaac Newton's Life* (London: Taylor and Francis, 1936), p. 57.

2. Richard S. Westfall, *Never at Rest* (Cambridge, England: Cambridge University Press, 1980), p. 209.

3. Ibid., p. 281.

Chapter 6. A Question of Gravity

1. Richard S. Westfall, *Never at Rest* (Cambridge, England: Cambridge University Press, 1980), p. 383.

2. Gale E. Christianson, *In the Presence of the Creator* (New York: The Free Press, 1984), p. 237.

Chapter 7. The *Principia*

1. Isaac Newton, Translated by I. Bernard Cohen and Anne Whitman, *The Principia, Mathematical Principles of Natural Philosophy* (Berkeley: University of California Press, 1999).

2. Gale E. Christianson, *In the Presence of the Creator* (New York: The Free Press, 1984), p. 291.

Chapter 8. Outside Forces

1. Gale E. Christianson, *In the Presence of the Creator* (New York: The Free Press, 1984), p. 321.

2. Ibid., p. 325.

3. Ibid., p. 356.

4. Richard S. Westfall, *Never at Rest* (Cambridge, England: Cambridge University Press, 1980), p. 196.

Chapter 9. The Mint

1. H. D. Anthony, *Sir Isaac Newton* (London: Abelard-Schuman, 1960), p. 139.

2. Ibid., p. 146.

3. William Stukeley, *Memoirs of Sir Isaac Newton's Life* (London: Taylor and Francis, 1936), p. 14.

Chapter 10. "The Great Ocean of Truth"

1. Richard S. Westfall, *Never at Rest* (Cambridge, England: Cambridge University Press, 1980), p. 583.

2. Ibid., p. 869.

3. Ibid., p. 870.

4. Ibid., p. 863.

Chapter 11. "On the Shoulders of Giants"

1. John Fauvel, Raymond Flood, Michael Shortland, and Robin Wilson, eds., *Let Newton Be!* (Oxford, England: Oxford University Press, 1988), p. 38.

2. Isaac Newton, Translated by I. Bernard Cohen and Anne Whitman, *The Principia, Mathematical Principles of Natural Philosophy* (Berkeley: University of California Press, 1999), p. 408.

3. Ibid.

Glossary

alchemy—The forerunner of modern chemistry. Alchemy blended science and magic.

binomial—A mathematical equation with two elements, such as 2x + 3y.

calculus—The branch of mathematics invented by Isaac Newton. It is used to determine, for example, the area under a curve.

ellipse—A flattened circle, or oval.

fellowship—A position to which a graduate of a university may be elected.

fluxions—The name used by Isaac Newton for calculus, the branch of mathematics he invented.

geometry—The branch of mathematics dealing with lines, flat shapes (e.g., circles and squares), and solid shapes (e.g., spheres and cubes).

gravity—The attraction or pulling force between one object and another.

inverse-square law—As two objects get farther apart, the force of attraction between them weakens by one divided by the square of the distance between the objects. This can be written as $1/d^2$, where d is distance.

law—A scientific principle that is universally accepted as fact.

mass—The amount of matter in an object. Mass is different from weight, which depends on gravity. You would weigh less on the moon but your mass would still be the same as on earth.

optics—The study of light.

plague—An epidemic of disease, where the rate of death is very high.

prism—A multisided piece of glass or crystal.

reflecting telescope—A telescope that uses two mirrors to give a clearer vision.

sizar—A student at Cambridge University who worked at the university in order to pay for his room and board.

spectrum—The colors that make up white light. To humans, the visible spectrum is red, orange, yellow, green, blue, indigo, and violet.

theory—A general term for a scientific principle that has been proved by experimentation.

Further Reading

Books

Allan, Tony. *Isaac Newton*. Oxford: Heinemann Library, 2002.

Krull, Kathleen. *Isaac Newton*. New York: Viking, 2006.

Mason, Paul. *Isaac Newton*. Austin, Tex.: Raintree Steck-Vaughn, 2001.

Parker, Barry. *The Mystery of Gravity*. Tarrytown, N.Y.: Benchmark Books, 2003.

Purdie Salas, Laura. *Discovering Nature's Laws: A Story About Isaac Newton*. Minneapolis: Carolrhoda Books, 2004.

Internet Addresses

Isaac Newton
http://www.pbs.org/wnet/hawking/cosmostar/html/cstars_newt.html

Newton's Three Laws of Motion
http://csep10.phys.utk.edu/astr161/lect/history/newton3laws.html

Sir Isaac Newton: The Universal Law of Gravitation
http://csep10.phys.utk.edu/astr161/lect/history/newtongrav.html

Index

K

Kepler, Johannes, 37–39, 64, 75, 100, 102

L

Leibniz, William, 35–36, 93
London, 30–31, 44, 46, 50, 64, 68, 81, 85, 87–89, 91, 94–95, 1120

M

Mathematics, 6, 13, 22–24, 32, 34–35, 40, 47, 57, 59, 69, 72, 103
Maxwell, James Clerk, 104
Mint, 84–88, 90–91, 93

N

natural philosophy, 71
Newton, Isaac,
    career changes, 47, 82, 84, 90
    childhood, 5–6, 8–16
    death, 97
    education, 9–10, 13, 19–24, 27, 46–47
    health, 5, 83–64, 95, 97
    knighthood, 94, 108

P

Parliament, 13–14, 80–82, 87
Pepys, Samuel, 28, 31, 44, 52, 73, 83
physics, 12, 36, 71
plague, 30–31, 46–47
Principia, 69–71, 73–74, 77–78, 91

R

Royal Society, 28–29, 50, 53, 60, 65, 71, 73, 91, 94–95, 97

S

Smith, Barnabas, 8, 10, 21
Smith, Hannah Newton, 5, 8, 10, 16, 19, 21, 62–63
Storer, Arthur, 10, 14, 64
Storer, Edward, 10, 62, 64
Storer, Miss. 10–11
Stukeley, William, 11, 27, 34, 94

T

telescope, 6, 41, 47–51, 92
Trinity College, 20–21, 54, 77, 94, 96

W

Wickins, John, 21–22, 54, 57, 84
Woolsthorpe Manor, 6, 8–10, 17, 21, 27, 32–33, 47, 62, 70, 88
Wren, Christopher, 28, 64–65, 57, 112